zing!

*five steps and 101 tips
for creativity on command*

By Sam Harrison

MacHillock Publishing
Highlands, North Carolina

International Standard Book Number: 0-9744996-3-3

Library of Congress Control Number: 2003111332
Library of Congress Cataloging-in-Publication data
Available from Library of Congress

1st Printing, 2004

08 07 06 05 04   8 7 6 5 4 3 2 1
Printing Code:
The rightmost double-digit number is the year of the book's printing
The rightmost single-digit number is the number of the book's printing.
Printing code 04-1 denotes that the first printing occurred in 2004.

Cover and interior design by Lamar Ussery
Selected photography by Cyr Smith

For more information, visit www.zingzone.com or email sdh@mindspring.com

With appreciation

– to Lamar Ussery for designing this book.
A close friend and remarkable designer,
Lamar has made me look much better
than I deserve for many years.

– to Cyr Smith, an all-around virtuoso
and valued friend, for his fine photography.
All good photos in the book are Cyr's.
The rest are mine.

– and most of all,
to Hope, my wife and star.

zing!

"Stung by the splendour
of a sudden thought."

Robert Browning

"There is a vitality, a life force, an energy, a
quickening that is translated through you
into action…"

Martha Graham

"There's a way
to do it better. Find it."

Thomas Edison

zing! *contents*

What's *zing!* about?

It's about creativity and curiosity. Passion and punch. Vitality and velocity. It's about getting to the point. Fast.

Many books formalize creativity into humdrum, weighing down the topic with sluggish suppositions. Even more books on creativity are at the other end of the scale, beating around the bush with a bunch of silliness and sounding like geese on nitrous oxide.

Zing! darts between those two extremes.

In your hands is a smart, five-step process for finding creativity when you need it. But rather than bore you with tired theories, this definitive guide explains those five steps with a pastiche of pithy examples, tips and tools. Everything except witchcraft to kick-start your creativity.

You can dole out the doses one at a time – perhaps one a day. Or you can roar through the pages like fire licking up hay. Either way, you'll get a synaptic boost to offset gravitational tugs of dullness. You'll discover fresh ideas. And you'll have fun along the way.

As you journey through this book, you'll probably hear the high-pitched sounds of bold thoughts zinging around your brain. Because *zing!* is all about inspiration, energy and action. About cutting through the clutter and delivering the goods. About a five-step process to help you find ideas well before the deadlines.

Are you ready to zing?

And what's the five-step process?

Let's be clear here: every idea doesn't require a process. We've all had uncountable ideas that popped out of nowhere. And may they pop forever.

But we've also had those angst-filled days when deadlines loomed near and ideas steered clear. And we've all been on creative teams that spun around in more circles than terriers chasing tails.

Those are times for a process – a methodology – for creativity on command.

There's no formula for creativity. No cookie-cutter solution. But there is definitely a flowing form in the way highly creative people glide toward exciting, endless ideas. And you can tap into such a process to find rich and abundant ideas.

Many people and organizations rely on step-by-step processes – stated or unstated – to zing them toward inspiration. This is especially true for those having to come up with ideas on a deadline: ad agencies, design studios, PR people, meeting planners, product developers, freelancers, columnists and scores of others.

In fact, about the only people who look askance at creative processes are those who haven't tried one.

Before us are five steps for having ideas when you need them. And lots of stories, tips and tools to bring those steps to life. In this small book, we've packed in everything you need to zing.

Then let's start zinging.

Creative zing
is about
exploring
freedom,
embracing life.

Zing is about:
finding history in markets
rather than in museums

finding inspiration in cafés
rather than on computers

finding insights in diaries
rather than in demographics

Zing is about:
getting off expressways and
heading out pathways

meeting new people and
spending time with old people

knowing nine to five is just one-third
of total creative time

Zing is about:
laughing rather than whining

reaching out rather than holding in

going to the edge rather than
staying stuck in the middle

*It's all about exploring freedom,
embracing life.*

And that's our process for creative zing:

Explore Freedom, Embrace Life

1. Explore

o b s e r v e   a n d   r e s e a r c h

2. Freedom

b r a i n s t o r m   a n d   v i s u a l i z e

3. Comma

p a u s e   a n d   d e t a c h

4. Embrace

e d i t   a n d   s e l e c t

5. Life

p r o t o t y p e   a n d   i m p l e m e n t

Try the steps on for size.

Step 1: Explore

It begins with deep digging. You're the excavator. Archaeologist. Explorer. You peek under the mundane to find the magical. Others can sit at desks and study demographics. You sit at Starbucks and study people. Others search archives. You search antique shops.

You haul up buckets of data and information, but you're mining for insights. You don't just want ages, genders and zip codes. You want to know about their theme songs, water-fountain gossip and favorite hangouts. You don't just want to hear about personality sets. You want to know what makes them laugh, cry and scream. You stop, look and listen. You explore.

Step 2: Freedom

Then you throw open your mind's shutters and let the wind rush in. You brainstorm. Doodle. Think. Play. Daydream. You have a free-range brain.

No judging. No opinions. No clucking of tongues. Down the road you'll edit down your stack of ideas. Right now, you're after quantity, not quality. You're going wild.

Step 3: Pause

Ahhh, you come up for air. Unhunch your shoulders. Let go. Get the conscious mind out of the way. Your subconscious is yelling for elbowroom. It needs workspace.

You take a walk. Go to a movie. Meet a friend for lunch. You slack off while your subconscious sweats. Good deal, huh?

Step 4: Embrace

OK, break's over. Time to rock and roll. While you were back there goofing off, your subconscious was doing the heavy lifting. Now the brightest idea floats before you. Aha! There it is.

Step 5: Life

You tap on the water glass and get everybody's attention – it's time to sell. You draw sketches, write drafts, build prototypes. Add flesh and bones. Beat the drums. "Listen up!" you shout. "I've got a great idea here."

You verify the idea. Tinker to make the whole thing better. Talk the white out of the moon until people listen. Pick up a few selling tips from your brother-in-law, the software hawker. You slap backs. Sweet-talk. Schmooze.

You pace floors. Knock on doors. Wear a sandwich board on main street if you have to. But you don't give up until the idea comes to life. You bring that baby to life.

That's the creative process.
Feels good, doesn't it?

zing!

This book now breaks into five sections –
one for each step. Within each section are words
and tools to make the creative process
resonate for you.

Proceed at your own pace.
Read straight through if you like.
Or take it a day at a time, one page each morning.
And keep the book handy for quick shots of
inspiration, plucking out quotes and examples
whenever creativity needs a jolt.

With this easy handbook, you don't have to sift
through hundreds of pages to find precious
nuggets. Key points are right before your eyes.
No fluff. No fooling. Just *zing!*

Step 1.

Explore

"I go to encounter for the millionth
time the reality of experience."

James Joyce

Become a sponge.

Ian Schrager and Philippe Stark collaborated on designing boutique hotels like the Clift in San Francisco and the Hudson in New York.

"Whenever we start a project, we're both voyeurs," says Schrager. "We take in information like a sponge."

Exploring is about asking questions and absorbing insights.

Make a list of 50 questions for a project you're about to begin.

"People only see what they are prepared to see."

Ralph Waldo Emerson

Look in places you don't usually look.

Listen with intent.

Carry a notebook.

Ray Bradbury is the author of more than 500 published works – short stories, novels, stage plays, screenplays, TV scripts, poetry.

Exploring became his oxygen and the secret of his prolific creativity. Bradbury told Jack Foster that he had read a short story, an essay and a poem every day since childhood.

Feed Your Mind All The Time.

"If you stuff yourself full of poems, essays, plays, stories, novels, films, comic strips, magazines and music," Bradbury said, "you will automatically explode every morning like Old Faithful. I have never had a dry period in my life because I feed myself well."

**Make an exploration list for your life.
Fill it with readings, films, music.**

Notice people. Lots of people.

Christopher Guest, director and star of *Spinal Tap,* *Best of Show* and *Waiting for Guffman*, gets his ideas by watching and listening to other people.

Sitting in a hotel lobby, Guest overheard a discombobulating exchange between members of a second-rate rock band. *Spinal Tap* was born.

Best of Show came about after Guest watched dog owners fussing over their four-legged babies in a park near his home.

And *Waiting for Guffman* characters are composites of people Guest watched in high school and college theaters.

"Before anything else," says Christopher Guest, "I would describe myself as an observer."

Go out of your way to observe people today.

Zing is fast but not rushed.

Anticipate.

Several years ago, Rodney Dangerfield was phoning me from time to time about a product idea. I didn't see much potential, so after three or four calls, I said: "I gotta tell you, Rodney, there's little hope or money in this product. Why are you so interested?"

A pause followed, and I could visualize him tugging his collar, as in his comedy routines. After a moment, he said, "It's not the money, Sam, it's the anticipation. Anticipation is the greatest thing in life."

I don't totally agree – there's much to be said for the pleasures of in-the-now moments – but anticipation does provide powerful zing.

List three projects or activities you're looking forward to:

1. _____

2. _____

3. _____

Use the zing of anticipation to spark ideas.

ideas ARE HERE, THERE, and EVERYWHERE.

In Atlanta for daughter Stella's fashion show, Paul McCartney found himself with a free afternoon. But rather than sit in front of a TV, McCartney took to the streets, exploring the fringes of downtown. He discovered an old drugstore that stocked folk medicines and was mesmerized by their catchy names.

The name of one remedy, "Run Devil Run," eventually became the title song for his rock-and-roll CD.

Visit new places, find new ideas.

Are you looking for ideas in the same old places?

TURN OFF TV.
TURN ON MIND.

"I find television
very educational.
Every time someone
switches it on,
I go into
another room
and read a
good book."

G r o u c h o   M a r x

ARE YOUR EYES HUNGRY?

For years I was involved in a joint venture with John Denver and his environmental groups. One morning as we walked along a stone path near his Windstar property, I asked how he created songs.

"I just watch what's going on around me and write about it," he said. "Hiking in the mountains, I write about trees. Falling in love, I write about romance. Fishing in Alaska, I write about that scenery. Songs are written with the eyes as well as the ears."

When our eyes are hungry, our imaginations get fed.

Don't just look. See.

What touches you will touch others.

When sculptor and architect Maya Lin was a student at Yale, the names of alumni killed in Vietnam were carved on a wall in Woolsey Hall. She couldn't resist touching those names as she walked past.

When Lin's class entered a national design competition, she remembered those chiseled names. A similar feature emerged in her design. Maya Lin won the competition, and for more than two decades, millions have run fingers across carved names on the Vietnam Veterans Memorial in Washington, D.C.

Notice your reaction to textures, sounds and images.
If something inspires you, it will likely inspire others.

Small details determine whether your creativity
whispers or **roars.**

When Samuel Wright accepted the role as Mufasa in "Lion King," he wanted to find the perfect growl. So he spent hours at Bronx Zoo, watching and listening to lions. In time, he discovered the growls came not from the lions' throats but rather from their soft palates, which amplify vibrations. Mimicking this technique, Wright developed a valiant roar for every performance.

List five interesting details in one of your projects or ideas:

1. _____

2. _____

3. _____

4. _____

5. _____

Select one detail and conduct eyes-and-ears research.

Own a pair of subway ears.

Waiting in a Colorado ski-lift line, I overheard a woman telling her friend, "I was so free I felt as if I were wearing ballet slippers."

I don't know if she was describing her last ski run or the end of her last relationship, but the imagery stuck in my head. Having never worn ballet slippers, I wouldn't think to utter such a line. Later that day, I scribbled the sentence in my notebook. And I've already used it in a short story and a marketing piece.

Active listening can be a lodestone for new insights and ideas. Billy Crystal came up with *City Slickers* after hearing two people recalling their dude-ranch adventures. E.L. Doctorow, author of *Ragtime* and *World's Fair*, talks about the value of "Subway Ears" – extending our listening antennas in crowds.

Tune in to surroundings and gather new material.

"All speech is a dead language unless it finds a willing and prepared listener."

Robert Louis Stevenson

ARE YOU LISTENING OR JUST WAITING TO TALK?

An old theater joke says a narcissistic actor reviews a script like this:

> "Blah, blah, MY LINE! blah, blah, MY LINE! blah, MY LINE!...

Hard to admit, but in conversations I've sometimes been like that self-absorbed actor. Maybe you have too. From time to time, we all seem to regard listening as the space we endure before speaking again. Tongues wag and ears rest.

Listening takes effort but leads to great ideas. When Frank Perdue decided to get in the chicken business, he first took a job in a supermarket so he could listen to customers. When people told him they bought chicken based on its appearance, he grabbed market share by offering plump, cleaner poultry.

**Listen to what people have to tell you.
You might be surprised.**

Listening List

Talk with five new people this week. Ask simple questions. Listen to what they have to say. Write down your insights.

Today I really listened to _____

I learned _____

Today I really listened to _____

I learned _____

Today I really listened to _____

I learned _____

Today I really listened to _____

I learned _____

Today I really listened to _____

I learned _____

Look until you connect.

Creativity asks us to look closely and deeply.
Only then can we capture the essence of what we're observing.

Rodney Smith, an accomplished photographer in New York,
creates fine art as well as commercial work for a stellar list of clients.

A short lens is always on Smith's camera, because he wants to remain
close to his subjects. He slowly moves around the person or object until
he feels an emotional connection.

And at that moment, he clicks the shutter.

**When exploring today, give your
eyes time to capture.**

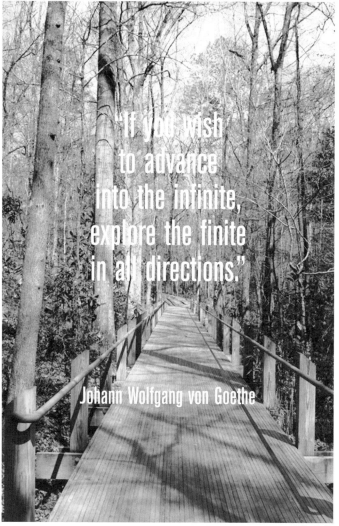

"If you wish
to advance
into the infinite,
explore the finite
in all directions."

Johann Wolfgang von Goethe

©Cyr Smith

What Would Nature Do?

The business world is filled with examples of biomimicry, the study of how nature can be imitated to solve problems.

A Swiss hiker noticed cockleburs clinging to his pants and invented Velcro. John Todd studied natural filtration in wetlands and developed a revolutionary water-purifying system.

Patagonia, the outdoor-clothing firm, studies feather and fur – natural insulators – for ideas on designing warmer jackets.

Nike designers observed mountain goats at the Oregon Zoo to develop Goatek Traction, an all-terrain shoe.

Look at your creative problem and ask:

"What would nature do?"

"We should learn
to approach
the natural world
as a library of ideas
rather than
a warehouse
of materials."

B a r r y   M .   K a t z

Zing is terriers, not toads.

Leave the Closed World, explore the Green World.

Green World and Closed World are labels used by literary critic Northrop Frye when discussing Shakespeare's plays.

In Frye's lexicon, Closed World represents the court-life reality and convention of Elizabethan England. Green World is the changeable "forest" of nature, imagination and art.

Shakespeare's plays often conclude with characters returning to the Closed World after being inspired and enriched by the Green World.

Open your gates and explore the Green World of art and nature.

©Cyr Smith

Zing is seeing sideways and shooting but shooting straight.

Travel Blue Highways.

In seminars, I urge participants
to zing their creativity by traveling down life's
Blue Highways, Buford Highways and Lonesome
Highways.

Blue Highways are small, less-traveled roads
(traditionally shown in blue ink on road maps).

Travel the Blue Highways in your world
to shake up the scenery.
Take different routes to work.
Walk down unfamiliar streets.
Enter the mall through the back door.

Set yourself up to see fresh things.

Find Your Buford Highway.

In my hometown of Atlanta, Buford Highway
is a road known for wall-to-wall ethnic restaurants.
Within a two-mile stretch, you can choose between
Cuban sandwiches and Chinese dim sum,
Mexican tacos and Mongolian beef,
Indian curry and Indonesian noodles.

Your town or city probably has its
own version of Buford Highway.

Take that road tonight.

Eat something new.

Soak up the surroundings.

Cruise Down Lonesome Highways.

Lonesome Highways are room-for-one paths
to vivify our senses.

We tend to notice more details
when traveling alone, whether it's a
three-day business trip or
an afternoon at a coffee shop.

**Head out by yourself for an hour or for a week.
Notice people. Activities. Objects.
Record your findings.**

Zing is reaching out rather than holding in.

Solo Sightings

Travel alone to four public places this week.
Record what you see, hear and feel.

Today I got away to:

Here's what I noticed:

Today I got away to:

Here's what I noticed:

Today I got away to:

Here's what I noticed:

Today I got away to:

Here's what I noticed:

"The important thing is not to stop questioning. Curiosity has its own reason for existing."

Albert Einstein

Pick a project or problem that you feel you fully understand.

Now ask **10** more

questions about it.

©Cyr Smith

Zing is passionate rather than passive.

43

Sit in different classrooms.

To create poetic, esoteric music for millions of diehard fans, the **Grateful Dead** found teachers in unlikely places.

Bass player Phil Lesh studied with Italian composer Luciano Berio.

Guitarist Bob Weir was inspired by jazz pianist McCoy Tyner.

Jerry Garcia spent hours in bookstores and film houses.

Drummer Mickey Hart explored classical Indian drumming.

Lyricist Robert Hunter borrowed techniques from T.S. Eliot and Hans Christian Anderson.

List three sources of inspiration outside your discipline:

1. _____

2. _____

3. _____

Explore.

Observe with penetration.

A great book for your creativity shelf is *An Actor Prepares* by Constantin Stanislavski.

As the father of method acting, Stanislavski focused on stage techniques, but his sage advice applies to any creative explorer.

"An actor should be observant, not only on the stage but in real life," he writes. "He should concentrate with all his being on whatever attracts his attention. He should look at an object with penetration."

Is your vision bouncing off the surface?

Practice looking with penetration at least five times today.

Micro-managing limits creativity, but micro-looking expands it.

Micro-looking is the approach of Private Eye, a fascinating program that uses a jeweler's loupe to closely examine the world. The loupe blocks out distractions and alters how we ordinarily see things.

Loupe-looking at an object,
ask yourself questions, such as:

What does this remind me of?

Why does it look this way?

How could I use what I see?

Use micro-looking to study a painting, a product or nature. Or let it help you climb out of a brainstorming rut.

©Cyr Smith

Zing is jamming rather than living.

47

How does it sound, smell, taste, look, feel?

For best results, explore with all of your senses.

The legendary guitarist Les Paul learned this decades ago when he built his own electric guitar using telephone parts and a four-by-four.

Paul played his "log" – as he called it – at a New York nightspot. Sounded good to him, but the audience was underwhelmed.

The next day, Paul glued his contraption to the body of a Spanish guitar and returned to the same nightclub. The audience ate it up, and Paul discovered that people listen with eyes as well as ears.

Soft-drink companies have learned a similar lesson. In blind taste tastes, loyal customers often prefer a competitor's product. But attach a brand name and these same customers quickly change their preference. From these experiments, soda firms realized people use their eyes to "drink the can."

Be aware of all your senses —
and those of your audience.

STOP EXPLORING WHEN YOU'VE FOUND HEAVEN.

When researchers arrive at the Pearly Gates,
they face two doors:
the first says "Heaven," and the second says
"Research About Heaven." Out of habit, many
researchers choose the second door.

Like most virtues,
research can be exaggerated into vice.

Explore until it's time to stop.

{ **Then stop.** }

Step 2.

Freedom

"To have good ideas,
have lots of ideas."

Linus   Pauling

Squeeze and Release.

In the Explore Step,
we squeeze in all available information.
In the Freedom Step, we release every insight,
catapulting our minds toward the big idea.

With this step we give ourselves freedom
to brainstorm and daydream,
doodle and scribble.

**We open our minds
and welcome all ideas.**

"Let your thoughts
meander toward
a sea of ideas."

Leo D. Minnigh

Creative Explosions.

Deadlines sometime call for explosive creativity.

Such was the case with the Dave Matthews Band a few years ago when it was struggling to complete a new album.

Enter producer Glen Ballard, a protégé of Quincy Jones, who has worked with musicians from Alanis Morrisette to Aerosmith.

Ballard doesn't believe in sitting around and waiting for inspiration. He believes in finding it. Keeping the band in the studio, Ballard encouraged quick ideas and fast composition. The result was what he called an "explosion of creativity."

By "putting the pedal to the metal," as Dave Matthews termed it, the band created 10 album-worthy pieces of music in just nine days.

Is your brainstorming explosive?

"If you have **an apple**
and I have **an apple**
and we exchange **these apples**,
then you and I will still each have
one apple.

But if you have **an idea**
and I have **an idea**
and we exchange **those ideas**,
then each of us will have
two ideas."

G e o r g e   B e r n a r d   S h a w

**During the next week,
exchange ideas with these five people:**

1. _____

2. _____

3. _____

4. _____

5. _____

Brainstorming Rules.

Huh?

All this talk about freedom,
and now we're laying down laws?

Actually, these simple guidelines – derived from the suggestions
of Alex Osborn, father of brainstorming – will boost freedom
and inspire free-flowing ideas.

And by the way, the rules apply to both team and solo brainstorming.

I. JUDGE NOT

Brainstorming isn't the place to evaluate or edit ideas.
That comes later. The goal is to generate as many ideas as possible.
Crazy suggestions often spark great solutions.

II. GO NUTS

Encourage yourself and others to offer any idea,
no matter how wacky. It's quantity, not quality with brainstorming.

III. FOCUS

Go nuts, but stick to the topic.
And the floor goes to one person at a time.

IV. JAM

Imitate jazz musicians. Play off of each other's ideas,
adding riffs and improvisations.

"An idea is delicate.
It can be killed by
a sneer or a yawn;
it can be stabbed to death
by a joke or worried to death
by a frown on the
right person's brow."

Charles Brower

JUDGE NOT.

Fresh thoughts seldom brew in an atmosphere
filled with:

"it won't work"

"we've tried
that before"

"what a dumb idea"

The Freedom step isn't about
the perfect idea. It's about lots of ideas.

One hundred ideas an hour is what IDEO strives
for in its spirited and productive sessions for
product development.

Your brainstorming won't spawn multiple ideas —
and certainly not revolutionary ideas — if fresh
thoughts gets slammed against the wall.

©Getty Images

"Every really new idea looks crazy at first."

Alfred North Whitehead

How loud is your Internal Broadcasting System?

Each of us has an internal broadcasting system.
And sometimes it's tuned to the
Negative News Network:

People will laugh at me.
Who do I think I am?
This idea will never work.

Michael Ray calls this network the "voice of judgement."
Gail Goodwin says it's the "watcher at the gates."
John Hershey labeled it the "censor of the mind."

Call it whatever, but be aware of your Negative News Network.
It's usually reporting from unreliable sources.

©Cyr Smith

Pull the plug on your Negative News Network.

1. Listen up.

Hear what NNN is saying and keep a journal. Gail Goodwin even draws pictures of her "watcher at the gates."

2. Write a letter.

Fire off a complaint about the programming to your NNN. Burn or delete when you're done.

3. Speak up.

Find a private spot and literally outshout your NNN. Tell it to shut up and move on.

4. Exercise.

Negative News Network hates jogging, yoga, tennis — even short strolls through the malls.

5. Look around.

NNN also abhors exploring. There's no room in its agenda for new books, ethnic foods, clever shops. Be curious, and Negative News Network will experience technical difficulties.

"Our doubts are our traitors."

Shakespeare

What doubts are holding you back?

1. _____

2. _____

3. _____

4. _____

5. _____

Put these traitors on trial.

©Cyr Smith

Everybody's got problems.

Woody Allen is one of the most independent of filmmakers, seemingly untouched by Hollywood.

Yet Allen says that each time he makes a movie, "the truck bearing compromises eventually arrives at the door," forcing him to face budgeting details, actors' schedules and location hassles.

Regardless of our status, difficult circumstances will come knocking.

The challenge is to be **creative** *regardless of conditions.*

Creativity dwells above the murk.

I once ran into a wise old friend, and he asked how I was doing.

"Fine, under the circumstances," I replied.

He raised his eyebrows and laughed:

"What, pray tell, are you doing under there?"

**What circumstances are you under?
List three moves you can make
to rise above those conditions.**

1. _____
   _____

2. _____
   _____

3. _____
   _____

Assume nothing is impossible today.

"Impossible is a word to be found
only in the dictionary of fools."

Napoleon Bonaparte

"It's kind of fun to do the impossible."

Walt Disney

"There's no use trying," said Alice.
"One can't believe impossible things."
"I daresay you haven't had much practice,"
said the Queen. "When I was your age,
I always did it for half an hour a day.
Why sometimes I've believed as many as
six impossible things before breakfast."

Lewis Carroll

"Go ahead and
do the impossible.
It's worth the look
on the faces of those
who said you couldn't."

Walter Bagehot

NO SOFT TOSS ALLOWED

Put some zing in your delivery: pitch a few fastballs and change-ups.

The world doesn't want to hear about the labor pains.

It just wants to see the baby.

Close your account
at the Excuses Exchange.

A proud sponsor of Negative News Network
is the Eveready Excuses Exchange.
Its shelves are packed with handy evasions:

I'm too busy.

I don't have enough money.

I don't have enough education.

My boyfriend won't like it.

My wife doesn't understand me.

The client is stupid.

I'm so tired.

Enough already.

BURN YOUR BOATS.

Caesar and other ancient warriors burned their boats when invading countries. Seeing their flaming ships behind them, armies realized they must conquer or die.

No alternatives. No excuses.

Jack Foster, author of *How To Get Ideas*, recommended taking a cue from Caesar and learning to burn our excuses:

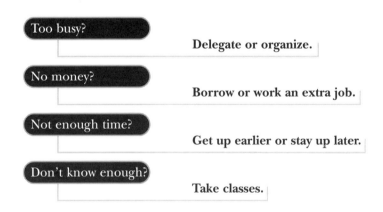

Too busy?
Delegate or organize.

No money?
Borrow or work an extra job.

Not enough time?
Get up earlier or stay up later.

Don't know enough?
Take classes.

START
THE FLAME.

But:	So:

**In the box, name a project you've
delayed with excuses.
List your excuses in the left column.
In the right column, list actions you'll take
to burn those excuses.**

"Learn **not** to be careful."

Diane Arbus

©Cyr Smith

Override Your **RAS**

At the base of the brain sits a clearinghouse called the Reticular Activating System. The RAS helps decide what information is important. It filters out some messages and magnifies others.

In a way, it serves as an early-warning device. Its survival instincts often magnify negative messages and downplay positive ones.

"Be careful" is the RAS motto.

Such caution can, of course, be life-saving in truly dangerous situations, but also a constant block to creative freedom. Don't let the RAS scare you away from risks inherent to new ideas.

Identify a project where you've been overly cautious. Ignore the Be Careful signposts and move full speed ahead.

"I am always doing that which I can not do in order that I may learn how to do it."

Picasso

76

What telescopes are you avoiding?

When the telescope was invented in the 1600s,
Galileo used the new device to study planets.
He soon found errors in existing theories.

Fellow scholars scoffed, so Galileo asked them
to peer through the telescope themselves.

Most refused to look.

At times, we're all guilty of such blindness.
Comfortable with preconceived notions
and old ideas, we close our eyes to
new possibilities.

"The problem is never
how to get new,
innovative thoughts
into your mind,
but how to get
the old ones **out**."

Dee Hock

"COLOR WITHIN THE LINES."

"COPY SHOULD
SOUND THIS WAY."

"MEETINGS ARE
SERIOUS BUSINESS."

"BUSINESS LETTERS SHOULD
BE FORMAL."

"DESIGN SHOULD BE
TRADITIONAL."

"WE DON'T DO IT THAT WAY."

FIXED OPINIONS

Identify three fixed opinions in your world:

1. _____

2. _____

3. _____

Ignore them!

"Great spirits
have always
encountered
violent opposition
from mediocre
minds."

Albert Einstein

Play on new M-Fields.

Downhill racers once feared an 80-miles-per-hour run was too fast. But when that barrier was broken, skiers feared 80 mph was too slow.

Dr. David Hawkins uses "M-Fields" to describe such changes in our field of consciousness (he borrows the term from Sheldrake's morphogenetic fields).

Roger Bannister created a new M-Field when he broke the four-minute mile. People had assumed an under-four-minute mile was impossible. Aware of Bannister's M-Field, other runners soon broke the barrier.

©Cyr Smith

Humans crash into new paradigms and M-Fields are created. The Wright brothers with flight. MacIntosh with user-friendly computers. Bernbach with his disarmingly honest Volkswagen ads.

Where can you create a new M-Field?

"The creative mind plays with the objects it loves."

C a r l   J u n g

Think of six ways to make a current project more playful:

1. _____

2. _____

3. _____

4. _____

5. _____

6. _____

Possess a playful lingo.

Zap! Zoom! Whip! Spin! Flip!

The lexicon of action figures is also the language of creative heroes.
On following pages, we'll talk about how these
playful but powerful words can zing your creativity.

Post these words in your workspace.

ZAP!

ZOOM!

WHIP!

SPIN!

FLIP!

ZAP!

If you're struggling with a problem, try zapping – eliminating or reducing elements to arrive at a solution.

A major brokerage firm was mailing a series of inexpensive items to its best customers – things like paperweights, pens and coasters. We were asked to review the campaign, and a survey confirmed our suspicions: the frequent mailings were meaningless to the affluent customers. They tossed or gave away the cheesy gifts.

Zap! We eliminated the mailings and used the same budget to create handsome leather portfolios that were hand-delivered by account managers. Recipients still talk about this successful campaign.

There's impact in simplicity. Look at Japanese cuisine, Tiffany's jewelry, French films.

Zapping superfluous elements often creates elegant solutions.

ZOOM!

If zapping isn't the answer, maybe zooming is.

Zoom out to enlarge one or more elements. That's the strategy of big-box retailers like Target, Home Depot and Wal-Mart. And it's the idea behind products like Jolt Cola (double caffeine) and DirecTV (mega-channels).

Artist Jeff Koon zoomed to create a 40-foot puppy decorated with thousands of flowers at Rockefeller Center.

Pike Place Fish Market zoomed by taking its workers' quirky habit of tossing fish and making it a major tourist attraction.

And Goodby, Silverstein & Partners – recognizing that certain foods taste better with milk – zoomed that notion into the famous "Got Milk?" ad campaign.

Zoom your way to creativity by enlarging an element or idea.

86

WHIP!

Whip together two or more existing elements and see what happens.

Edison connected a toy funnel and the motions of a paper doll to invent the phonograph.

Barbara Kruger whips together provoking words and dramatic type to create unique works of art.

Reese's combines chocolate and peanut butter.

Crest blends toothpaste and mouthwash.

Chiat/Day combined a pink bunny with pitches for phony products to whip together the unforgettable Energizer ad campaign.

What existing ideas can you whip together?

SPIN!

Spin an existing idea into new directions.

Kitty litter was just for cats until somebody found it also helped motorists stuck on icy roads.

BreatheRight strips were just for congestion until Jerry Rice discovered they could help athletes get more oxygen while on the playing field.

Baking soda was only for cooking until Arm and Hammer spun the product in new directions – first as a refrigerator refresher and today as an ingredient in toothpaste, deodorants and air filters.

What old ideas can you
spin in new directions?

Flip your idea over, inside out, upside down. Operation Opposite.

That's what Oprah did when she looked at Jerry Springer's mean and messy talk show, then flipped her show in the opposite direction.

That's what Steve Jobs and Steve Wozniak did when they looked at the complexity of computers and invented ready-to-use machines.

And flipping is what Dave Eggers did when he decided to launch a literary magazine. Rather than resort to the moss-worn, academic look of most literary publications, Eggers flipped the genre on its highbrow head with *McSweeney's* magazine.

McSweeney's is fresh every time. One issue is a box filled with short stories in their own booklets. Another is a book with a CD of original music to accompany the stories. Recipients eagerly await each issue, because they know Eggers won't settle for sameness.

Are you following the crowd or doing what's been done? Take a U-turn and head in the opposite direction.

"You can't wait for creativity. You have to go after it with a club."

J a c k L o n d o n

BE A TEAM PLAYER.

As a Chicago Bull, Michael Jordon
once scored 69 points in a game.

Afterwards, reporters were lined
up to interview the great star,
so one sportswriter took a different slant.
He walked over to a rookie player
who had scored one point.

"What do you think of all of this?"
asked the reporter.

"Well," said the rookie, "I'm just proud that
Michael Jordan and I worked together
tonight to score 70 points."

*Give all you've got
and share the credit.*

"Without ice cream, there would be chaos and darkness."

Don Kardong

Ideas flow faster when ice cream or
Krispy Kremes arrive at the brainstorming session.

And idea-saturated firms always seem to have
break rooms stocked with candy, sodas and fruit.

Maybe it's the sugar rush.
Perhaps the psychology of rewards.
But whatever the reason,
treats add zing to creativity.

What If?

**"What if?" is a popular tool
for generating ideas, creating designs, solving problems.**

What if a personal computer was fun and easy to use?
asked Steve Jobs and Steve Wozniak, and the result
was Macintosh.

What if a hub-and-spoke system was used for overnight delivery?
asked Fred Smith, and the result was FedEx.

What if a beer bottle looked really different?
asked Interbrew, and the result was Wildbrew in a tiger-print bottle.

Hundreds of "What if?" questions
can be asked to inspire creative thinking:

What if a child had this problem?
What if a dog had this problem?
What if money wasn't a consideration?
What if I had to have an answer in 10 minutes?
What if this was twice as big or half the size?

And on and on...

©Cyr Smith

"Nothing is new except arrangement."

William Durant

O + C = I

Visiting a South African diamond mine, Paul Simon noticed a fine powder on the miners' shoes. He realized it was diamond dust.

The observation stayed with Simon, and he soon connected it with music. This provided a song idea for his *Graceland* album, the classic "Diamonds on the Soles of My Shoes."

Observations + Connections = Ideas

Put observations to work.

After watching the workings of a coin punch and a wine press, Guttenberg invented the printing press.

After observing bored parents and their kids at a run-down playground, Walt Disney created Disneyland.

After seeing a candy bar melt in his pocket while he stood in front of a magnetron, Percy Spencer invented the microwave oven.

Are you connecting the dots in front of your eyes?

Make 10 fresh observations this week.

1. _____
2. _____
3. _____
4. _____
5. _____
6. _____
7. _____
8. _____
9. _____
10. _____

**Can you apply these
observations to existing projects?**

NO MORE SEQUELS.

*"The real difference between New York and L.A.
is that in New York everyone in every industry
is looking for the next new idea.
In L.A., everyone just wants to make the sequel."*

Thomas Bezucha, movie director

Playing it safe and settling for
copycat solutions suffocates zing.

Barry Sternlicht, creative director for
W Hotels, instructs his designers to find
ways to surprise their guests.

**When we surprise ourselves and others,
we stop making sequels and start making
blockbusters.**

"I DWELL IN POSSIBILITY."

Emily Dickinson

Step 3.
Pause

"I waited for the ideas to consolidate,
for the groupings and composition
of themes to settle themselves
in my brain."

M o n e t

Comma = Pause.

And the comma in
Explore Freedom, Embrace Life
expresses the Pause Step of the creative path.

Rollo May said inspiration happens
when the subconscious is stimulated by hard work,
then freed by the rest that follows.

Einstein said his best ideas came while shaving.

Pause = Incubation
A time for the subconscious to zing
while the conscious mind detaches.

"A hunch is creativity trying to tell you something."

Frank Capra

Pause often.

_____

Keep notebooks handy.

_____

Record every hunch.

BLACK MIRRORS FOR YOUR MIND.

After working with intense colors, early Impressionist painters
soothed their eyes by gazing into "black mirrors"
that mimicked dark pools.

The pause also gave the conscious mind a break and let the
subconscious clock in. Artists returned to their canvases with
rejuvenated eyes and fresh perspectives.

Find your own black mirrors – quiet walks or short naps,
ping-pong or softball, conversations or movies. Anything that
removes you from the project at hand and gives your
subconscious a chance to work.

Creativity can't stand to struggle.

Give it a rest.

The pilot's voice crackled through the intercom:
"Ladies and gentlemen,
I have good news and bad news.
The bad news is we're lost.
The good news is we have a
200-mile-an-hour tail wind."

Bumper sticker seen recently:
"I may be lost, but I'm making record time."

**Are you busting butt to finish a project
that's likely heading down the wrong path?**

Pause and get your bearings.

Fish in an idea stream.

Songwriters sometimes sit and write a song
from start to finish, seemingly without effort.

Arlo Guthrie, who's experienced this phenomenon
more than once, says he feels there's a stream of songs in the universe,
and a songwriter just has to know when to reach out and grab one.

"I'm just glad I don't live downstream from Bob Dylan," he adds.

Pause at least
three times today.

Accept all ideas in your
stream of consciousness.

"WITHOUT GREAT SOLITUDE NO SERIOUS WORK IS POSSIBLE."

Picasso

DISCONNECT FROM ALL THE CHATTER.

In 1990, five-million Americans used cell phones.
Today, 140 million use them.

They're ringing away in meetings, restaurants and bars.
Even in libraries, health clubs and churches.

And cells are just one way people reach out and grab us.
We're also connected by land phones,
e-mails, faxes, pagers and voice mails.

Whew.
And we wonder what happens to creative think time?

Specify 30 minute time slots during which you'll unplug from all communications technology:

Clear Time # 1

Clear Time # 2

Clear Time # 3

©Cyr Smith

"All of man's troubles stem from his inability to sit quietly in a room alone."

Pascal

Find a convenient hideaway.
Escape often.

111

Pause like a diver on a springboard.

Don't confuse the Pause Step with laziness
or passivity.

Pausing comes only after the robust Explore
and Freedom steps.

Pausing demands alertness, Rollo May explained
in *The Courage to Create,* as when a diver is balanced
on the end of a springboard, waiting for the right
moment to move.

Stand ready to leap!

"Don't say that you don't have enough time. You have exactly the same number of hours per day that were given to Helen Keller, Pasteur, Michelangelo, Mother Teresea, Leonardo da Vinci, Thomas Jefferson and Albert Einstein."

H. Jackson Brown Jr.

Step 4.
Embrace

"Genius is the ability to edit."

Charlie Chaplin

Everything clicks.

"The click" is what Ray Gregory, professor at the Royal College of Art, calls the ignition occurring when he gets the perfect idea.

That's the Embrace Step –
reaching out and grabbing a golden idea.
Sometimes it comes through conscious
editing or culling.
Other times it's the joyful discovery
of something there all along.

"When I am working on a problem,"
said Buckminster Fuller,
"I never think about beauty. But when I have
finished, if the solution is not beautiful,
I know it is wrong."

**With the Embrace Step,
we find a solution that zings.**

Mihaly Csikszentmihalyi,
prominent professor and author of *Creativity*,
says that during the Embrace Step,
or what he calls the Aha! experience,
a solution becomes all but inevitable.

A RELEASED CORK.

He compares an insight charging into our awareness
to a cork hitting the surface
after being released from underwater.

**Use pocket notebooks
to capture popping corks.**

"Creativity is
allowing yourself
to make mistakes.
Art is knowing
which ones
to keep."

*Scott Adams,
creator of* Dilbert
comic strip.

Chip Away.

Great ideas often surge from the mind like Csikszentmihalyi's cork. When that happens, gratefully embrace those ideas and go forward.

But times also come when corks don't pop to the surface. When that happens, we must consciously edit down thoughts and insights generated during the Freedom Step.

Remember what Michelangelo said when asked how he was able to carve something as astonishingly beautiful as his statue of David: "The statue's shape already exists in the marble. I simply chip away the excess stone."

©Cyr Smith

BECOME A RUTHLESS EDITOR.

Following the Freedom Step, you'll have lots of ideas.

Good and bad.
Serious and silly.
Costly and cheap.

The Embrace Step is the time to edit down those ideas.
A time to sit on the bench and become a ruthless judge.

I often suggest that people put aside their first three ideas,
because those will likely be the same ideas others would have.

Strive for something different. Fly past sameness.

Eliminate anything standing in the way of great zing.

The good is often the enemy of the best.

Make courageous calls.

The legendary University of Alabama coach,
Paul "Bear" Bryant,
once called for a quarterback sneak on
the last play of a close game.
The play failed and Alabama lost.

The next weekend, a reporter cornered Bryant and said:
"Coach, I wouldn't have run that
quarterback sneak last Saturday."

"Yes, and if I had had a week to think about it,"
said Bryant,
"I wouldn't have either."

**Make decisions when they're needed.
(And avoid Monday-morning quarterbacking.)**

"In any
moment of decision,
the best thing
you can do
is the **right** thing.

The **worst** thing
you can do
is nothing."

Theodore Roosevelt

Step 5.
Life!

"Nothing great is accomplished
without enthusiasm."

Emerson

Breathe life into your idea.

In this step, you add flesh,
bones and heart to your idea.
And you make it lively and likable.

Likable?
Yes, because we must become
salespeople for our ideas.
Nobody's ever been bored into buying anything.

Steve Jobs is a Life Step genius.
When he and Steven Wozniak developed the first
Apple computer, Jobs brought the product to life
with his pitchman skills.

And when introducing Macintosh in 1984,
Jobs created a gladiator image for his baby,
selling it as a revolutionary, counter-culture
alternative to colossal, traditional computers.

Read books or listen to tapes on selling skills.
One resource I recommend in my seminars
is "The Psychology of Selling" by Brian Tracy.
www.briantracy.com

"In the modern world of business, it is useless to be a creative, original thinker unless you can also sell what you create. Management cannot be expected to recognize a good idea unless it is presented to them by a good salesman."

David Ogilvy

Scale down the approval party.

When presenting ideas, show limited options.
If you give lots of choices, you'll get nit-picking
and meandering. Focus instead on selling
your **best** ideas.

Also limit the number of decision-makers in
the room. Two or three is ideal, and never more
than six. Otherwise, approvers will swarm over
your ideas, burying them with raging egos, turf
battles and split hairs.

**Before showing ideas,
plot out your presentation.**

Solicit conspirators.

The hostess of a formal dinner party approached Winston Churchill and told him a prominent earl had lifted one of her antique salt shakers. Churchill tucked a similar shaker in his own dinner jacket, then pulled the man aside. "I think we've been spotted," said Churchill, opening his pocket to give the earl a peek. "We'd better put these back."

People tend to cooperate with fellow conspirators. In fact, the word conspire originally had less sinister connotations, meaning "breathing as one." Sure, it takes time and energy to involve decision-makers in the creative process. But the payoff is priceless. When decision-makers and idea merchants "breath as one," final sign-offs become mere formalities.

Who makes those life-or-death decisions on your ideas? Conspire with them throughout the creative process.

Pick your battles.

Nobody likes working with someone who declares
war on every issue. If you're that person, chill.
Don't waste energy and goodwill battling over
each and every detail.
Instead, recognize the tipping points
(places where small changes spark significantly
different results) and fight for critical ones.
Graciously concede other points. You'll be viewed
as flexible and accommodating – and you can use
those small concessions to negotiate go-aheads
on true tipping points.

**Do you come out with guns
blazing over every objection or change?
Decide which details are really worth
powder and cannon balls.**

In Aristotelian philosophy, entelechy
is the condition of a thing whose essence is fully realized.

In today's lingo, that means moving from potential to
actuality. A powerful word for creativity and the Life Step.

Entelechy existed when Johnson & Johnson
saw the potential of gauze-and-tape bandages
and invented Band-Aids.

Entelechy = Life Step

Entelechy existed when Tom Wolfe and Truman Capote
saw the potential of storytelling in true events
and wrote the non-fiction novels
The Right Stuff and *In Cold Blood.*

Entelechy exists when Richard Avadon and Annie Leibovitz
see potential in human faces
and create magnificent photographic portraits.

**Entelechy exists when
you see potential in ideas
and zing them into life.**

Drill until you find oil.

Oil magnate J. Paul Getty was once asked

to write a short piece explaining his success. He wrote:

Some people find oil.

Some don't.

That pretty much sums up creativity.

Some people tap into their creative resources. Some don't.

Some people enhance ideas with the help of others. Some don't.

Some people bring ideas to life. Some don't.

Keep drilling until your idea gushes with life.

Make a list of five ideas you've been sitting on:

1. _____

2. _____

3. _____

4. _____

5. _____

Move before somebody else does!

"Even if you are on
the right track,
you will get run over
if you just sit there."

Will Rogers

©Cyr Smith

"To avoid criticism, do nothing, say nothing, be nothing."

Elbert Hubbard

As we bring ideas to life, somebody is sure to criticize.

When Manet tried showing his paintings in a private gallery,
the public scoffed and critics slammed his work.

The Paris Salon rejected his first paintings,
as well as many subsequent works.

To have his paintings shown at the Paris World's Fair in 1867,
Manet had to build a pavilion with his own funds.
He paid to be insulted.

And when *Olympia*, his nude on satin pillows,
was finally accepted by the Paris Salon,
crowds jeered and spit at the exhibit.

Only in his later years,
with the birth of Impressionism,
did Manet begin to receive positive recognition.

Don't let criticism zap your zing.

"The **dread** of criticism is the **death** of genius."

William Gilmore Simms

Be on guard for any attack.

When we present ideas to others,
we'll often encounter pushback.

Tough questions.
Dyspeptic criticism.
Downright rejection.

Missiles will be fired, and ducking isn't a viable strategy.

**Anticipate objections
and prepare to counter.**

Prepare a missile defense system.

Missile Defense System

PROJECT: _____

Missile _____   Defense _____

Before presenting your next idea, create this form.
Under *Missile*, list possible objections and questions.
Under *Defense*, articulate your responses.
You'll deliver a stronger and more self-confident pitch.

Want to meet for dinner?
I'll try.

Tommy, will you cut the grass before I get home?
I'll try.

Can you come up with a great idea by tomorrow?
I'll try.

Wanna bet money on those commitments?
Probably not.

Because "I'll try" usually signals lack
of wholehearted effort.

TRY = Timidly Resisting Yes

Take "try" out of your vocabulary.

BECOME A TINKER.

A century back, tinkers traveled from village to village, mending metal utensils. But today's tinkers are creative thinkers. Often we hear a creator say, "I just kept tinkering until I got it right."

When Alfred Butts lost his job during the Depression, he invented Lexico, a game where players constructed words from nine tiles. Parker Brothers and Milton Bradley rejected his idea. Butts kept tinkering.

He added a board and gave point values to each letter. Game companies rejected him again. Butts kept tinkering.

He went to seven tiles and gave points to squares on the board. And he teamed with James Brunot, who changed Lexico's name.

In 1952 – 20 years after Butts' idea – Macy's placed a giant order. And within two years, five million Scrabble sets were sold.

List three projects in your dead file that tinkering might resuscitate:

1. _____

2. _____

3. _____

"Once you learn to quit, it becomes a habit."

Vince Lombardi

Don't quit too soon.

President Reagan often told the story about an American
guy who went to Italy to study opera.

After a few years, he was invited to sing at La Scala.
They were performing Pagliacci, and he sang the aria,
Vesti La Giuba.

He received lengthy applause, so he repeated
the aria as an encore.
Again, great applause and again he sang *Vesti La Giuba.*

This went on and on, until finally he motioned for quiet.
"I'm grateful," he said, "but exhausted. I have sung *Vesti la
Giuba* nine times now. My voice is gone.
I cannot do it again."

And a voice from the balcony shouted,
"You'll do it until you get it right!"

Seymour's Fat Lady

Remember "Seymour's Fat Lady" in *Franny and Zooey?*

When Franny and Zooey were kids appearing on the radio show, "It's a Wise Child," their older brother, Seymour, would admonish them to shine their shoes or say something funny on the show.

He would tell them to do it for the Fat Lady "sitting on this porch all day, swatting flies, with her radio going full-blast..."

The notion of Seymour's Fat Lady has meaning for all who create products, art or communications.

When we fall into the rut of working by the numbers and wondering who really cares, we can remind ourselves to add something special for Seymour's Fat Lady – the one person out there who desperately needs what we have to say, show or sell.

**During the Life Step, add extra zing to your efforts.
You never know who you'll touch.**

"Any activity
becomes creative
when the doer
cares about
doing it right
or doing it better."

John Updike

Pick the right time to sell ideas.

We learned this strategy as kids. We didn't ask Dad about that new bike until after his second cup of coffee. And before hitting up Mom for extra allowance, we made sure she'd had a good day at work.

Nothing's really changed. If you want approvals to go smoothly, know what's on the calendars and minds of decision-makers. Are you showing on a day when the misery index is high? Is your presentation wedged between a financial audit and global conference call? Is the key decision-maker enduring a 24-hour fast before her colonoscopy?

Talk with administrative assistants and other contacts long before your presentation. Make sure the coast is clear. If it's not, be flexible about shifting to a more harmonious time.

When bringing ideas to life, don't rely on luck.

Once your idea is sold, don't buy it back.

I once worked with a fellow who was great at pitching ideas. Mike was smart, articulate and passionate, but he didn't know when to sit down and shut up.
When he showed ideas, clients would applaud, cheer and practically wave currency in his face. But Mike wouldn't let that stop him; he just kept right on talking. And the more he talked, the more those decision-makers reconsidered. After a few painful we-had-'em-then-lost-'em episodes, Mike finally learned to stop when decision-makers were ready to buy.

Leave your audiences begging for more rather than begging for mercy.

Afterword

Well, here you are. At the end of the five-step process.
But, of course, it's really the start of Exploring Freedom,
Embracing Life.
The next step is up to you. Test the efficacy of *zing!*
Take its suggestions into your workplace and personal life. Play
around with the methodology. Test the brainstorming tips.
Notice the Negative News Network. Work hard.
Take breaks. Leap from good to best. Shout from roofs.
Have fun.
We were born to manifest the glory that is within us, said
Nelson Mandela. My hope is that *zing!* will help manifest the
light inside of you. Your creativity is craving freedom. Let it out.
Let it zing.

Warm thoughts,

Sam Harrison

"Think in the morning. Act in the noon.
Eat in the evening. Sleep in the night."

W i l l i a m   B l a k e

Suggested Reading

Aha! by Jordan Ayan
Life's Little Instruction Book by H. Jackson Brown
I Am Almost Always Hungry by Cahan and Associates
The Other 90% by Robert K. Cooper
The 7 Habits of Highly Effective People by Stephen R. Covey
Lateral Thinking by Edward deBono
Creativity, Conversations With 28 Who Excel by Susan Charlotte
Creativity by Mikaly Csikszentmihalyi
How to Get Ideas by Jack Foster
Creating Minds by Howard Gardner
The Creative Process by Brewster Ghiselin
Power vs Force by David R. Hawkins
Infinite Mind by Valerie V. Hunt
Rousing Creativity by Floyd Hurt
Mistakes That Worked by Foltz Jones
Notebooks of The Mind by Vera John-Steiner
Jamming by John Kao
The Art of Innovation by Tom Kelly
The Act of Creation by Arthur Koestler
Thinkertoys by Michael Michalko
Thinking for A Living by Joey Reiman
The Fall of Advertising and The Rise of PR by Al Ries and Laura Ries
Orbiting the Giant Hairball by Gordon MacKenzie
99% Inspiration by Bryan W. Mattimore
LifeStyle by Bruce Mau
The Courage to Create by Rollo May
The Creative Edge by William C. Miller
The Five Faces of Genius by Annette Moser-Wellman
The Pursuit of WOW! by Tom Peters
Creativity in Business by Michael Ray and Rochelle Myers
Collaborative Creativity by Jack Ricchiuto
Serious Play by Michael Schrage
An Actor Prepares by Constantin Stanislavski
Hey, Whipple, Squeeze This by Luke Sullivan
Chemistry by Stone Yamashita Partners
Goals! by Brian Tracy
Whack on the Side of the Head by Roger Von Oech
Five Star Mind by Tom Wujec
The Art of Thought by Graham Wallas
A Technique for Producing Ideas by James Webb Young
Fast Company Magazine @www.fastcompany.com
HOW Magazine @ www.howdesign.com
I.D. The International Design Magazine @ www.ID-Mag.com
McSweeney's Quarterly @ www.mcsweeneys.net
Metropolis Magazine @ www. metropolismag.com
STEP @ www.dgusa.com

End Notes

4   "There is a vitality…" a quote from Martha Graham in *Dance to the Piper* by Agnes DeMille, DaCapo Press 1980

17   "Whenever we start…like a sponge." "Masters of the Zeitgeist," by Martin C. Pedersen, *Metropolis,* 1/02

19   *How To Get Ideas* by Jack Foster, Berrett-Koehler Publishers, Inc. and www.raybradbury.com and www.spoerlein.iwarp.com

20   "Before anything else…observer." New Yorker Literary Festival, 5/01

26   *The New Yorker,* "The Reluctant Memorialist," by Louis Menand, 7/8/02

27   *The New York Times,* 8/17/01

32   see images by Rodney Smith at www.kodak.com and www.ephotozine.com

34   *I.D. Magazine,* "Design Evolution," by Barry M. Katz, 5/02

36   *A Natural Perspective,* by Northrop Frye, Columbia University Press, 1993, and www.darwilliams.com & www.darwilliams.net

44   *The New York Times Book Review,* "Do Not Speak Ill of the Dead," by Will Hermes (review of *A Long Strange Trip,* by Dennis McNally) 8/2/02

45   *An Actor Prepares* by Constantin Stanislavski, Theater Arts, New York

46   www.the-private-eye.com. website of The Private Eye Project

48   NPR News Morning Edition, "Present at the Creation," by Christopher Joyce, 8/12/02

55   www. cbsnews.com, "Inside the Dave Matthews Band," from "60 Minutes II," 1/23/01

72   *How To Get Ideas* by Jack Foster, Berrett-Koehler Publishers, Inc.

75   *The Other 90%* by Robert K. Cooper, Crown Business, New York

78   *Fast Company,* Oct./Nov., 1996, by M. Mitchell Waldrop

82   *Power vs. Force* by Dr. David R. Hawkins, Veritas Publishing

89   *McSweeney's Quarterly* @ <u>www.mcsweeneys.net</u>

92   "Without...darkness." "Pyramid Scheme," by Don Kardong,
          Runner's World, 7/02

94   <u>www.willdurant.com</u>, website of Will Durant Foundation

98   "The real difference...the sequel." *The New York Times,* "O vanity,
          Where Is Thy Sting, Men Try Los Angeles," by David Colman, 4/14/02

103   *The Courage to Create,* by Rollo May, W.W. Norton & Company,
         New York

108   "I'm just glad...Bob Dylan." NPR segment by Marika Partidge on
         Pat Humphries and her song, "Swimmng to the Other Side," 5/22/02

112   *The Courage to Create,* by Rollo May, W.W. Norton & Company,
         New York, *A Smile for the Mind,* by Beryl McAlhone & David Stuart,
         Phaidon Press Ltd, London

113   *Life's Instruction Books* by H. Jackson Brown, Rutledge Hill Press, visit
         <u>www.instructionbook.com</u> for product information

117   *A Smile for the Mind,* by McAlhonee and Stuart, Plaidon Press

118   *Creativity,* by Mihaly Csikszentmihalyi, Harper Perennial, New York

130   Ogilvy quote recalled by Brian Collins, executive creative director,
         Ogilvy & Mather

131   Information for this page as well as pages 132, 133, 148, and 149 first
         appeared in *HOW Magazine,* December 2003, in an article by the
         author, "Prepare for Creative Combat."

138   *The People's Almanac,* by David Wallechinski and Irving Wallace,
         Doubleday and Company, Inc., Garden City, New York

143   NPR, "Present at the Creation," reported by Stefan Fatsis, 8/19/02,
         www.npr.org

146   "sitting on this porch...going full blast..." *Franny and Zooey,* by
         J. D. Salinger, Little, Brown and Company, Boston

About the Author

Sam Harrison has more than 20 years of experience in creative communications. He headed creative services and brand communications for an S&P 500 firm and has worked with such clients and associates as NFL, Major League Baseball, Hallmark, Microsoft, Hasbro and John Denver Environmental Groups.

Sam lives in Atlanta where he teaches writing classes and creativity sessions at a graduate-studies program focused on creative communications. He also consults and provides frequent seminars and keynote talks to firms, associations and conferences across the country. sdh@mindspring.com or www.zingzone.com

About the Designer

Lamar Ussery is creative director and partner with Virtual Magic, a creative design and multi-media firm in Atlanta. Lamar has been creating award-winning work for Fortune 500 companies for more than 18 years. Outside of creating effective design and playing music, his passion in life is being with his wife Lisa and boys Austin and Taylor. clussery@bellsouth.net

About the Photographer

Cyr W. Smith is best known for his paintings, having exhibited for years in the United States and in galleries in Paris and throughout France. He has lived all over the US and in Europe and Asia. "I am always searching for insights and enjoying the creative process," he says, and his photography adds another facet of creative expression. "The approach has always been to simplify the subject matter, to capture the creative moment of recognition." cyr@biltmorecomm.com

ZING BACK!

We hope you've enjoyed *zing! five steps
and 101 tips for creativity on command.*
If you have ideas, stories or examples to pass along,
or if you'd like to share how this book worked for you,
please write or email us.

If you are interested in our
zing-related talks and seminars,
we would also love to hear from you.

You can contact us at:
Sam Harrison
Box 942296, Atlanta, GA 31141
sdh@mindspring.com or visit
www.zingzone.com